MW01002902

What America Owes the Jews,
What Jews Owe America

Toby

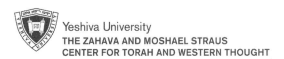
Yeshiva University
THE ZAHAVA AND MOSHAEL STRAUS
CENTER FOR TORAH AND WESTERN THOUGHT

WHAT AMERICA OWES
THE JEWS,
WHAT JEWS OWE AMERICA

Straus Center for Torah and Western Thought
The Toby Press

What America Owes the Jews, What Jews Owe America

The Toby Press LLC
POB 8531, New Milford, CT 06776–8531, USA
& POB 2455, London W1A 5WY, England
www.tobypress.com

© The Straus Center for Torah and Western Thought 2017
What America Owes the Jews, What Jews Owe America
ebook copyright © by Mosaic Books 2016

Cover image: Courtesy NYC Municipal Archives

ISBN 978-1-59264-474-2, *hardcover*

A CIP catalogue record for this title is
available from the British Library

Printed and bound in the United States

Contents

vi

Preface

With the exception of the chapters contributed by Jeffrey S. Gurock and Tevi Troy, the essays in this book were originally presented as talks at a conference titled "What America Owes the Jews, What Jews Owe America." The resulting ebook, published by Mosaic Books, is available in all major ebook formats.

The conference, held at Congregation Shearith Israel in New York City on Sunday, May 31, 2015, was sponsored by the Zahava and Moshael Straus Center for Torah and Western Thought of Yeshiva University, and was presented in partnership with *Mosaic* magazine and the Tikvah Fund. Meir Soloveichik, director of the Straus Center and rabbi of Congregation Shearith Israel, presided. William Kristol, editor of the *Weekly Standard*, moderated the proceedings. Eric Nelson, a professor of government at Harvard University and the author of *The Hebrew Republic*, contributed remarks, not included here, on "Hebraism and the American Founding."

Preface

Yeshiva University and the Straus Center wish to express their gratitude to Benjamin and Lynda Brafman and J. Philip and Malki Rosen for their generous support.

The publisher is grateful to Mosaic Books for permission to reprint the chapters contained in its ebook edition of *What America Owes the Jews, What Jews Owe America*. For more information, please visit *mosaicmagazine.com/books*.

Special thanks to the Straus Center, and in particular Stuart W. Halpern, Alan J. Secter, and Elina Mosheyeva, for their assistance in conceiving, organizing, and managing the conference, and thank you as well to the team at *The* Toby Press, and to Nechama Unterman, for their characteristic diligence and care in producing this volume.

For more information about the Zahava and Moshael Straus Center for Torah and Western Thought of Yeshiva University, please visit *yu.edu/straus*.

Adams, Jefferson, and the Jews

Meir Soloveichik

To what extent was the American idea founded on faith, and on the Hebrew Bible, and to what extent was it a product of reason, of philosophy, of natural law?

To put it slightly differently, to what extent was the American Revolution an achievement of Judaism?

Strikingly, this question would be answered very differently by two Founding Fathers: Thomas Jefferson and John Adams. They were, as Joseph Ellis writes in *Founding Fathers*, the odd couple of the revolution: "Adams, the highly combustible, ever combative, mile-a-minute talker…Jefferson, the always cool and self-contained enigma." It was Jefferson who composed the words of the Declaration that changed the world, but Adams was "the man…who sustained the debate, and by the force of his reasoning demonstrated not only the justice, but the expediency of the measure."

The two were the best of friends until the end of the eighteenth century, when they turned into rivals, and then ultimately enemies, before being reconciled in 1808 and beginning one of the great correspondences in American history. One issue that came up in their letters was religion in general, and Judaism in particular. Jefferson was long a hero to Jews; they were greatly indebted to his single-minded defense of religious freedom. And yet his own views of historical Judaism, and of the contributions and temperament of the Jewish people, remained negative, indeed virulently so. Adams, on the other hand, had great admiration for the Israel of the Bible and for the rabbinic tradition. This is interesting in its own right; but I would suggest that their disagreement on this matter actually relates to their different worldviews more generally.

Let us begin with a brief analysis of the beliefs of Adams and Jefferson. In their dogmas and doctrines they may have seemed similar, as they both called themselves Unitarians – that is, believers in God who denied traditional Christianity's notion of the Trinity. But Jefferson was essentially a deist; in his scheme, as the historian Richard Samuelson put it in *Commentary*, "God was the creator of the universe...but the idea that God was an active presence in the world he dismissed as mere superstition." Indeed, though Jefferson's Declaration of Independence did mention rights endowed by our Creator, the phrase at the end of the Declaration, invoking a "firm reliance on the protection of divine providence," was not in his original draft but was inserted by the Continental Congress. Jefferson, as an adult, never prayed. For him, reason and only reason was to serve as man's guide.

Adams, while also a great believer in human reason, adhered strongly to the importance of religion in forming a moral life, and especially so in a democracy. If the power of the state was to be vested in the will of the people, then nothing prevented the populace from running morally amok except their own self-restraint. Whereas Jefferson once wrote that the American mission was "to show by example the sufficiency of human reason for the care of human affairs," Adams, for his part, wrote that "We have no government armed with power capable of contending with human passions unbridled by morality and religion…. Our Constitution was made only for a moral and religious people. It is wholly inadequate to the government of any other."

Where did biblical Judaism fit into these two divergent views? For Jefferson, who considered reason the foundation of all progress, biblical Judaism, which was founded on the doctrine of hundreds of divinely inspired commandments that must be obeyed, was the epitome of all that was wrong with religion. "The whole religion of the Jew," wrote Jefferson in a letter in 1820, "was founded in the belief of divine inspiration. The fumes of the most disordered imaginations were recorded in their religious code, as special communications of the Deity…. [T]he religion of the Jews, as taught by Moses," he wrote further, "had presented for the object of their worship a Being of terrific character, cruel, vindictive, capricious, and unjust," and "had bound the Jews to many idle ceremonies, mummeries, and observances, of no effect toward producing the social utilities which constitute the essence of virtue." Therefore, Jefferson asserted, biblical Jews were "a bloodthirsty race, as cruel and remorseless as the Being whom they represented as the family God of Abraham, of Isaac, and of Jacob, and the local God of Israel."

Jefferson, you might say, was not exactly a fan of Judaism's intellectual heritage. And yet here I can't help pausing to point to a delicious irony. About fifteen years ago, researchers began investigating Jefferson's genes and discovered a match between the Jefferson family chromosome and a male descendant of Sally Hemings, one of Jefferson's slaves. This is well known; less well known is that the same research led to another discovery: Jefferson's Y chromosome was of a genetic branch that is quite rare and that originates in the Middle East. As the *New York Times* reported:

> Michael Hammer, a geneticist at the University of Arizona, said he had compared the Jefferson Y chromosome with those in his database of Y chromosomes and found a perfect match to the Y chromosome of a Moroccan Jew.

It is indeed delicious to contemplate the possibility that none other than Thomas Jefferson himself was a genetic descendant of that same "bloodthirsty race, as cruel and remorseless as the Being whom they represented as the family God of Abraham."

But now for the Adams family. To them, it was an undeniable fact that there had been many nations of great achievement in antiquity, but the transformative idea of an omnipotent, just God had never occurred to those nations. John Quincy Adams, in a letter to his son, once wrote:

> The ideas of God entertained by all the most illustrious and most ingenious nations of antiquity were weak and absurd…. Thus far and no farther could human reason extend…. The blessed and sublime idea of God, the creator of the universe…is *revealed* in the first verse of the Book of Genesis.

And here is how John Adams put the same thought in a famous letter of 1812:

> England and France are the two nations to whom mankind are under more obligations than to any other except the Hebrews. I excepted the Hebrews for…I will insist that the Hebrews have done more to civilize men than any other nation. If I were an atheist…[and] believed that all is ordered by chance, I should believe that chance had ordered the Jews to preserve and propagate to all mankind the doctrine of a supreme, intelligent, wise, almighty sovereign of the universe, which I believe to be the great essential principle of morality and all civilization.

Moreover, Adams's admiration did not stop with the Bible. It extended to the rabbinic tradition as well. Responding to Jefferson's negative assessment of the rabbis, Adams wrote plaintively that he wished he had the time to "examine the Mishna, Gemara, Cabbala [Kabbalah], Jezirah [*Sefer Yetzira*], Sohar [Zohar], Cosri [*Kuzari*], and Talmud of the Hebrews," but the task "would require the life of Methuselah." For Adams, indeed, rabbinic tradition might show the errors made by Christianity. "[T]wenty cartloads of Hebrew books were burnt in France" in the Middle Ages, he wrote. "How many proofs of the corruptions of Christianity might we find in the passages burnt?"

This is not to suggest that Adams was anti-Christian, let alone that he was an adherent of Judaism. He was neither. But neither did he despise the traditionalists of either faith, or of other faiths. He strongly valued faith's role in society, and he recognized that not everyone would have the same religious beliefs as himself.

We are now able to understand how Adams and Jefferson's disagreement about Judaism was not unrelated but actually profoundly linked to their larger worldviews, and in particular to their falling-out over the French Revolution.

For his part, Jefferson praised the 1789 revolution as the natural successor to the American one and said that "rather than it should have failed, I would have seen half the earth desolated." Adams's view was altogether otherwise. Like Edmund Burke across the Atlantic, he refused to see the revolution in France as a moral parallel to the American. Instead, he insisted that, in a French society shorn of faith and tradition, the result would be tyranny: "Is there a possibility," he reflected in his *Discourses on Davila,*

> that the government of nations may fall into the hands of men who teach the most disconsolate of all creeds, that men are but fireflies, and that this all is without a father? Is this the way to make man, as man, an object of respect? Or is it to make murder itself as indifferent as...the swallowing of mites on a morsel of cheese? If such a case should happen...give us again the gods of the Greeks...give us again our popes and hierarchies...with all their superstition and fanaticism.

In the end, Adams's warnings about the French Revolution, like Edmund Burke's, proved prescient. And we today would be wrong to ignore the link between Jefferson and Adams's debate over the American Revolution and their debate over the French Revolution. Rabbi Jonathan Sacks insightfully notes that there have been four revolutions in modern times: the British and the American on one side, the French and the Russian on the other. In Britain and America the source of inspiration was the

Hebrew Bible. In France and Russia it was the great alternative to the Bible, namely the philosophy of, respectively, Rousseau and Marx. Britain and America succeeded in creating free societies, albeit not without civil war, but at least without tyranny and terror. The French and Russian revolutions began in a dream of utopia and ended in a nightmare of bloodshed and the suppression of the very human rights in whose name they were launched. Rabbi Sacks writes:

> Much – perhaps all – turns on how a society answers the question: who is the ultimate sovereign, God or man?… For the British and American architects of liberty, God was the supreme power. All authority was therefore subject to the transcendental demands of the moral law. For the French and Russian ideologists, ultimate value lay in the state…. [W]hen human beings arrogate supreme power to themselves, politics loses its sole secure defense of freedom…. Societies that exile God lead to the eclipse of man. (*The Jonathan Sacks Haggada*, "Collected Essays on Pesaḥ")

As America broke into two political parties largely around the issue of revolutionary France, Adams and Jefferson went from being friends to becoming bitter enemies. Jefferson, in a letter, caustically described his political opponents, the Federalists, as "circumscribed within such narrow limits, and their population so full, that their number will ever be the minority, *and are marked, like the Jews, with such a perversity of character*, as to constitute, from that circumstance, the natural division of our parties" (emphasis added). That Jefferson chose, apropos of nothing, to compare the Federalists to Jews is noteworthy; perhaps he saw a Jewish notion in the insistence on religion as essential to a moral political society.

Reconciled after 1808, Adams and Jefferson remained in close connection until July 4, 1826, when they both died, exactly fifty years to the day of the adoption of the Declaration: surely the greatest proof possible of the Providence that Adams accepted and Jefferson denied. John Adams's last words were: "Thomas Jefferson survives." Actually, Jefferson had passed away several hours earlier in Monticello, but Adams's words remain true: Jefferson does survive, and the words of the Declaration that he composed endure to this day.

Yet Adams survives as well. Jefferson had boldly predicted the end of all traditional religion in America – "I trust," he said, "there is not a young man now living in the United states who will not die a Unitarian" – but his death was followed by a second Protestant Great Awakening, as well as the growth, noted with wonder by Alexis de Tocqueville, of Roman Catholicism, and even a homegrown religion, known as Mormonism, now the fastest growing faith in the world.

Today this country is immersed in a debate over religious freedom that is connected in its own way to the debate of two centuries ago. Facing us is the question of whether religious communities can remain true to their traditions, or whether our resurgent secular culture will succeed in forcibly imposing its own values on those communities. That question is unresolved, but, at least for the moment, there are places within the United States that remain John Adams's America, and I, for one, thank God for that.[1]

---

1. In addition to the authors cited in this essay, I am indebted to Rabbi Zevulun Charlop's "God in History and Halakhah from the Perspective of American History," *The Torah U-Madda Journal* 1 (1989): 43-58.

Zionism and Americanism: What Brandeis Saw and Why It Matters

Rick Richman

At the dawn of the twentieth century, Zionism was an unappealing idea to Americans in general and to American Jews in particular. Today, of course, nearly the opposite is true: Americans of both political parties, gentiles and Jews alike, support the State of Israel, and – with the troubling exception of various universities and certain other institutions – it enjoys the approval of a vast majority of Americans and substantially all American Jews.

How did it happen? Certainly, the intervening horror of the Holocaust made it clear that the Jews needed a state. But the idea of a modern Jewish state long preceded the Holocaust. The success of Zionism was the triumph of ideas propagated, debated, and refined over the half-century before the Holocaust, and of the efforts of exceptional individuals who devoted their lives to the cause during that period, including – but by no means limited to – Chaim Weizmann, Vladimir Jabotinsky, and David Ben-Gurion.

American Zionism was related to the Zionism that emerged from Russia and Europe, but it was also significantly different. It was a subcategory of the set of beliefs known as "Americanism," a civil religion that aspired to extend freedom, equality, and democracy throughout the world. The merger of Zionism and Americanism would prove critical to the formation of Israel in 1948, and that decisive merger was largely the work of a single person, Louis Dembitz Brandeis: a secular American Jew, born and raised in Kentucky, who in his first fifty-five years had shown little interest in Jews and Judaism – and none in Zionism.

We can pinpoint the moment the merger occurred. In August 1914, with the outbreak of World War I, Zionists in New York established a "Provisional Executive Committee for General Zionist Affairs" to replace the World Zionist headquarters in Berlin, which could not lead a world movement on a continent divided by war. The committee chose as its chairman one of the country's most famous legal minds and one of its most eminent Jews, Brandeis. In his acceptance speech, the fifty-nine-year-old Brandeis said:

> I feel my disqualification for this task. Throughout the long years which represent my own life, I have been to a great extent separated from Jews. I am very ignorant in things Jewish.

The Zionist emergence of Brandeis in 1914 would later be described by another prominent American Zionist as "a real miracle." The story is fascinating in itself, but it commands our special attention today because of its relevance to the current controversies surrounding both Zionism and Americanism more than a century after Brandeis's landmark speech.

Louis Brandeis was born to parents who had emigrated from Prague in 1848 and had prospered in America. They gave their son no Jewish education; he never observed Shabbat, attended religious services, or celebrated Jewish holidays, nor, despite his substantial resources as an adult, did he ever give more than minimally to Jewish charities before 1914.

In his distance from Zionism in particular, Brandeis was hardly alone among prominent American Jews of the time, including highly affiliated ones. In 1897, the year after Theodor Herzl published *The Jewish State*, Rabbi Isaac Mayer Wise, the head of Reform Judaism in America, publicly disparaged Zionism, calling it a "new Messianic movement" that appealed to "the fantastic dupes of a thoughtless Utopia"; it was a "momentary inebriation of morbid minds" that would rob Judaism of its "universal ground." For his part, Brandeis spoke similarly in 1905 to the New Century Club in Boston. Praising the virtues of assimilation, Brandeis said there was "no place for what President [Theodore] Roosevelt has called hyphenated Americans... [including] Jewish-Americans," and that "[h]abits of living or of thought which tend to keep alive difference of origin...are inconsistent with the American ideal of brotherhood, and are disloyal."

The conversion of Brandeis to Zionism sprang from several sources, and biographers still debate which was the most important. But one of the most significant was surely a meeting, about an unrelated subject, with Jacob de Haas, who before moving to America had been Herzl's secretary at four Zionist Congresses. De Haas was the editor of *The Jewish Advocate* in Boston. At the end of an interview about a controversy involving insurance law, he asked Brandeis if he was related to Louis Dembitz, a legal scholar and early supporter of the Zionist movement, whom de Haas called "a noble Jew." Brandeis replied that Dembitz was his much-revered, now-deceased uncle. This led to an hour-long discussion about Zionism, the first of many between them, and soon Brandeis was researching it with the same legendary thoroughness that he brought to his legal cases.

We do not know everything Brandeis read as he studied Zionism, but we can surmise that it included *Rome and Jerusalem: A Study in Jewish Nationalism* by Moses Hess, and Leon Pinsker's 1882 pamphlet, *Auto-Emancipation*, both of which argued that the liberal dream of universal peace was a false palliative for the beleaguered Jewish people. He certainly read the Zionist essays of Ahad Ha'Am, and no doubt those of Max Nordau, who was both the most prominent international public intellectual and Herzl's closest associate at the turn of the century. All of these tracts were written with intellectual force, literary grace, and moral urgency, and linked a solution to the so-called "Jewish Question" with the political principle that had governed world thinking since the mid-nineteenth century: nationalism.

By 1915, in an address entitled "The Jewish Problem: How to Solve It," Brandeis himself was asserting that liberalism, despite its great achievements, had failed to eliminate anti-Semitism, even in the enlightened European countries that had extended formal equality to Jews. And as for "the misnamed internationalism which seeks the obliteration of nationalities or peoples" – that, he said, was "unattainable." He was also convinced that a Jewish homeland would be able to conduct experiments in democracy and social justice that larger countries could not easily undertake. In a remarkable conclusion, he declared that "[t]he Jewish spirit, the product of our religion and experiences, is essentially modern and essentially American," and that a Jewish homeland would further American ideals. "My approach to Zionism," he wrote,

> was through Americanism. In time, practical experience and observation convinced me that Jews were, by reason of their traditions and their character, peculiarly fitted for the attainment of American ideals. Gradually it became clear to me that to be good Americans, we must be better Jews, and to be better Jews, we must become Zionists.

For American Jews, America was *home*, not exile, and Zionism, if it were to connect with them, and with Americans in general, had to justify itself in American terms. Brandeis made the connection in a uniquely compelling way, and thereafter proceeded to contribute to the cause not only his name and his funds, but also his time, his eloquence, and his personal commitment. "He took over with zest and enthusiasm," wrote Louis Lipsky, later the president of the Zionist Organization of America, dominating the movement with "logic, tact, and infinite patience."

The ranks of American Zionists surged after Brandeis became their head in 1914, increasing fifteen-fold over the next five years. But the most historically significant part of the Brandeis story came in 1917, with the debate in Britain over whether to commit the government to the establishment of a Jewish national home in Palestine. Chaim Weizmann, the Zionist leader in London, had been discussing a declaration with the British government since the beginning of the war. Now, facing strenuous public opposition from a British Jewish elite fearful that Zionism would jeopardize their status as British subjects, Weizmann turned to Brandeis for help.

In 1917, Louis Brandeis was one of the closest confidants of President Woodrow Wilson, whom he had met only five years before for a private lunch and a meeting that extended all afternoon, in which Brandeis had set forth ideas that would form the basis of Wilson's "New Freedom" campaign and, ultimately, the agenda of his administration. Wilson appointed him to the Supreme Court in 1916.

In April 1917, as America entered World War I and the British army was advancing against the Ottoman Turks in Palestine, the British foreign minister, Arthur Balfour, visited Washington and met Brandeis at a White House lunch. A few days later, in a forty-five-minute discussion at the White House, Brandeis found Wilson supportive of a Jewish homeland, and Brandeis then met with Balfour twice more. In September, as the British Cabinet met to discuss a draft declaration on Palestine, Edwin Montagu, the only Jew in the government, spoke vehemently against Zionism and circulated a passionate anti-Zionist memorandum to the Cabinet. Weizmann cabled Brandeis that it would greatly help "if President Wilson and yourself would support [the] text," and cabled again in October, asking Brandeis "urgently...to lend us a helping hand just at this moment."

Brandeis wired Weizmann that, based on his talks with Wilson, the president was in "entire sympathy" with the draft declaration, and in mid-October Wilson himself passed a private message to the British supporting the declaration. It was issued two weeks later. The message, Weizmann wrote later, was "one of the most important individual factors" in breaking the deadlock. Nahum Goldmann, later president of the World Zionist Organization, wrote in his autobiography that without Brandeis's efforts, the Balfour Declaration "would probably never have been issued."

Americanism and Zionism would become the most successful "isms" of a century in which the others – Communism, fascism, National Socialism, and anti-Semitism – murdered millions. As David Gelernter has noted, it was Americans who uniquely insisted that freedom and democracy were appropriate not only for themselves and France, but for Afghanistan and Iraq; not only for Germany, but for Japan and Korea as well. And, with its support for the Balfour Declaration in 1917 and the UN partition resolution in 1947, and the instantaneous recognition of the Jewish state in 1948, Americanism was also critical to the creation of Israel, the most successful democracy of them all.

And Zionism? We need not rehearse its manifold triumphs to acknowledge the one most central to our theme here – which, simply stated, is that Israel, even while coping with continual existential threats from its first hours till today, became and remained the democratic laboratory Brandeis envisioned, and the living realization of both Jewish and American ideals.

Would Brandeis be concerned that Israel today is politically more right than left, and economically more capitalist than socialist? I think not. Along with his Zionism, Brandeis developed a total faith in democracy. When he began to practice law, he wrote later, he had believed that it was "awkward, stupid, and vulgar that a jury of twelve inexpert men should have the power to decide," and that he "trusted only expert opinion." But "the experience of life," he said, "made me democratic." In the same way, he would respect the political leanings and electoral results of a Jewish democracy, and would recognize as well that "the experience of life" is the prism through which economic theories must be evaluated.

It is much more likely that Brandeis would be concerned about contemporary *liberal* political thought, and the adherence of so many American Jews to a rigid "Torah of liberalism" that brooks no dissent and stifles new perspectives. The strength of Zionism was that it was never a monolithic ideology. It was always a tree with many branches, and its cultural, economic, religious, and political diversity invigorated it. In contrast, Brandeis would recognize the intellectual shallowness of twenty-first-century liberalism, and he would appreciate the critiques of liberalism's problematic relationship with the Jews in Ruth Wisse's *If I Am Not for Myself...* and Norman Podhoretz's *Why Are Jews Liberals?* Indeed, he might very well endorse their incisive conclusions.

Brandeis might also recognize in today's American Jews a version of his pre-1914 self – highly educated, liberal by instinct, living in unprecedented freedom, but lacking substantial knowledge even of their own century's Jewish history, much less the history of centuries prior. He might well assert that the Jewish community needs a new Jacob de Haas to urge it to study the history of Zionism and the lives of the many "noble Jews" who created a state.

The story of Louis Brandeis illustrates the historical debt that Zionism and Americanism owe each other: in the twentieth century, they formed the preeminent alliance of hope and freedom in the world, and they achieved their ideals in an extraordinary partnership. The story is not well known among contemporary American Jews, too many of whom are not unlike Brandeis during the first fifty-five years of his exemplary life. But they have – to borrow the words of Brandeis in his 1914 acceptance speech – a "treasure to cherish" and a "sacred movement" to sustain; they are the "trustees" of Jewish history, charged to "carry forward what others have, in the past, borne so well."

Toward a New American Jewish Language

Dara Horn

Ever since my first novel was published in 2002, I've often been invited to participate on panels with other authors whose works have dealt with Jewish themes – and every time, there's a moderator who asks the same question: "Do you consider yourself a Jewish writer?" Generally the other panelists respond by saying, "No, no, no, I'm not a Jewish writer," which makes me wonder why we're all sitting in a Jewish Community Center.

There are, of course, many conversations one can have about what makes someone a Jewish writer: Does it matter whether the writer is Jewish, or whether the characters are Jewish, or is it something about the so-called "sensibility"? But having participated in these panels for thirteen years, I actually have a definitive answer to this vexing question. What makes someone a Jewish writer in America today is their likelihood of being asked to participate in a panel during which they will be asked the question, "Do you consider yourself a Jewish writer?" By that standard, I think I qualify.

But my thoughts on this problem are a bit more nuanced, because in addition to being a Jewish writer, I also moonlight as a professional Jewish nerd, with a doctorate in Hebrew and Yiddish literature. And one thing you learn when you do a doctorate in Yiddish literature is that no one ever asked Sholem Aleichem, "Do you consider yourself a Jewish writer?" The reason no one ever asked him that question is not because Jewish identity for him was any less complex, but simply because if you ask that question in Yiddish, it grammatically doesn't make sense, because the word for "Jewish" in Yiddish is "Yiddish." So if someone were to ask Sholem Aleichem this question, his answer might be something like "Duh." This simple fact reveals a great deal about what Jewish literature predominantly was for centuries: being a Jewish writer, in the most basic sense, meant writing in a Jewish language. This doesn't mean there weren't prominent outliers in other languages. It simply means that the Jewish literary canon was largely defined by the Jewish languages in which it was written.

If you're a person who doesn't read much in other languages, you might fairly wonder why this matters. It matters because every language has an archaeology of belief built into it, which native speakers may not even hear. If I say to you in English, "Go the extra mile," I'm not thinking, "I'm quoting the Gospels!" but I am. If I say to you in English, "It'll happen for better or for worse," I'm not thinking, "I'm quoting the Anglican marriage ceremony!" but I am. There is an archaeological layer of belief in a language that rises to the surface every time someone sneezes. In Jewish languages, that layer comes from the Torah, the Talmud, the siddur, the liturgy, the thousands of years of ritual and commentary created to enact and understand a contractual relationship with God.

To give just one example: in a Sholem Aleichem story about an insurance fire, the author can use one of the several Yiddish expressions for this phenomenon, like "lighting Shabbos candles in the middle of the week." And in a Sholem Aleichem story about an insurance fire, that fire also can't be just a fire, because as the Israeli literary critic Gershon Shaked pointed out, every fire in Jewish literature is an echo of the destruction of the Temple. That's a lot of weight for an insurance fire, but the language is strong enough to support it, and whether or not the writer exploits it, the reference is inherent in the words. Some writers choose to engage consciously with this layer, some don't, but this is the literary substructure on which art is created in these languages, regardless of the subject of the art itself.

So instead of speaking about who is and who isn't an American Jewish writer, I'd like to go to the deeper level of the problem and examine two paths of American Jewish literature from the last century taken by two important American Jewish writers, and what the divide between those paths can tell us about the possibilities of American Jewish literature today. The two paths are really two literatures: one in Yiddish and one in English.

American Yiddish literature began its life as a European transplant, in some cases with the very same writers. Sholem Aleichem, for instance, traveled from Russia to New York and brought his characters with him, writing his last unfinished novel about a Jewish boy immigrating to America. But what's remarkable about Yiddish literature in America is that by the late 1920s, when large-scale Jewish immigration was shut down by the US government, the most talented writers were mainly writing poetry rather than prose. The Anglo-American literary tradition might lead us to believe that this was an upgrade, but the truth is that as Yiddish faded as a spoken language among American Jews, it became less available for writers hoping to create realistic works of fiction set in the United States. The vast majority of quality Yiddish prose works by American writers are set in Europe.

As a novelist, I can imagine the aching limitation the loss of a daily spoken language meant for these writers. But I don't have to imagine it. I can see the problem come alive in the career of Yankev Glatshteyn, who died in 1975 as the most brilliant and underappreciated of American Jewish writers.

There is no doubt in my mind that Glatshteyn was a genius. Born in Lublin, Poland, in 1896, he immigrated to New York alone at age eighteen, where his only American relative couldn't leave his sweatshop job long enough to meet him at the dock. He had the option of living a fully assimilated American life, learning English fluently enough to get into law school at New York University, but he dropped out after deciding to commit himself to a Yiddish literary career and published his first book of poetry at age twenty-five. His early poems are extraordinarily sophisticated language games on a par with T.S. Eliot or the prose of James Joyce: high modernism catapulted into Yiddish, with magnificent results. The problem is that if I were to share these magnificent results with the reader, it would take many pages just to explain all of his dance steps. Poetry is always impossible to translate, but in Glatshteyn's case, the translator would need to render not only the meaning of the words and their style and register, and then the references to his contemporary world of Yiddish, English, and Polish culture, but also the world of traditional Jewish texts – and not merely that world, but the specific way that world was understood by

Yiddish-speakers – and finally the words Glatshteyn invented along the way.

Consider, for instance, just the title of a poem called "*Tsum Kopmayster*." Even to read this two-word title, you first need to have seen the poem's first word, the German "*hopmayster*," and to know that it's a play on the word "*hoyfyid*," a "court Jew," and the layers of self-critical history behind that term. Then you need to recognize the pun from "*khormayster*," a choir-leader in a non-Jewish musical tradition. Then you need to recognize the play on the word "*kop*" for "head" to get the English word "head-master," appreciate the legacy of a Yiddish-speaking tradition where living in one's head was a benefit rather than a liability, and then finally appreciate that titling a poem "To the Choirmaster/Head-master/Court Jew" is also a pun on the biblical Hebrew "*LaMenatze'aḥ*" or "To the Conductor," announcing this poem as a brand-new ironic American psalm.

You see the problem here. By digging this deeply into the well of Jewish literature, Glatshteyn did what many other writers before him did a bit less consciously, which was to create an art form that could only work in a Jewish language, because the path to any writer's highest artistic achievement is to do the most with the best gifts you have. But when the Nazis took over across the ocean, Glatshteyn's playfulness disappeared, leaving behind the bare archaeology of belief. Here are just a few lines from his poem "Goodnight, World," published in 1938: "Good night, world / Big, stinking world. Not you but I slam the gate... / Good night. I give you, world, a donation of all my liberators. Take your Jesusmarxes, choke on their courage, drop dead over a drop of our baptized blood. / ...I'm going back to my *daledamos* (my four cubits), from Wagner's idol-music to *niggun*, to humming. I kiss you, cankered Jewish life. It weeps in me, the joy of coming home."

Here again is the same problem as the *"Kopmayster,"* only here the problem has emerged out of the language and into the poem's subject. American society today pretends to care about multiculturalism, about hearing "other" voices. But this is truly a brilliant voice that, as history has clearly demonstrated, no one but Jews can hear. That voice became sadder and more resigned as Glatshteyn survived his audience, writing into the 1970s for an American Jewish community that had lost not only its language but also its soul. His poem "Like a Mousetrap" describes, as he puts it, "a little *shul* on Long Island" where "the worshipers are small in number / there's room for God's glory / but no one knows whether God will stop by." In Glatshteyn's post-Holocaust Yiddish, the audience shrinks so small that even God can't be counted on to participate.

So there's path number one for American Jewish literature: a language rich enough to evoke thousands of years of that archaeology of belief, but no future potential. What, then, of the writers working in English, on path number two? English at least promises its writers a significant audience, something that Yiddish in America at the time of Glatshteyn's death no longer could. But for the person who considers herself a Jewish writer, it comes with costs of its own.

My Exhibit A in this category is Saul Bellow, who stands head and shoulders above every other American novelist of the postwar twentieth century. Readers always point to the first sentence of his third novel, *The Adventures of Augie March*, published in 1953, as evidence not only of Bellow's emergent genius but of how proudly he shoved aside the contemporary voices of his time: "I am an American, Chicago born – Chicago, that somber city – and go at things as I have taught myself, freestyle, and will make the record in my own way: first to knock, first admitted; sometimes an innocent knock, sometimes a not so innocent."

This book, far beyond its first sentence, is a celebration of a Jewish man's ability to announce himself to the world as an American on his own terms, and there's no denying its success, both literary and otherwise. But as an American Jewish writer born more than three decades after this was published, I read that first sentence and can't help hearing just how loudly this young author feels the need to say it. In my novels it would never occur to me to have a character resembling myself announcing to the world that she was an American, because that would be like having her announce to the world that she was a woman, or a person. As a fourth-generation American, I can tell you that only a child of immigrants needs to make that kind of claim. Such was the status of American Jewish writers in English in 1953, and given the pressures on that generation, it's no surprise that Bellow was among the first American Jewish writers to announce loudly that no, no, no, he was not a Jewish writer.

Of course he was, though within limits that Glatshteyn never experienced. Bellow was the first to translate Isaac Bashevis Singer from Yiddish into English, though in such a limited way that he had to have the Yiddish critic Eliezer Greenberg read it out loud to him, because his command of Yiddish did not extend to reading it. That story was "*Gimpel Tam*," or in Bellow's translation "Gimpel the Fool" – though "*tam*" is a word that doesn't mean fool but rather an innocent, the word used to describe the biblical Job. It's impossible to read Bellow's book *Seize the Day*, written shortly after he translated "*Gimpel Tam*," without seeing its main suffering character, Tommy Wilhelm, as an American *tam*, an American Job whose main spiritual loss is that American life has deprived him of the nobility

---

of everyday suffering. *Seize the Day* does not need to announce its Americanness, but its characters' Judaism, the impoverished Judaism of the mousetrap *shul* on Long Island, is irrepressible within it, and rises up in the novel's final scene as the *tam* experiences a revelation at a Jewish funeral home.

In Bellow's later books like *Herzog* and *Mr. Sammler's Planet*, the connection to the Jewish textual tradition announces itself, as it does in Glatshteyn's poetry, as an absence, a memory of childhood recalled in order to bring meaning to an adulthood overwhelmed with superficiality. In the midst of being cuckolded, for instance, Moses Herzog recalls being in Hebrew school, studying the passage in Genesis about Joseph and Potiphar's wife. References like these appear on every page or two. They aren't intended to make religion appealing, but rather to evoke a past and a commitment to something beyond one's own fulfillment, in an American setting where the past is viewed as a liability and self-fulfillment is life's only public goal. These references seem structural rather than decorative: they serve as a counterpoint without which the judgment of American culture in these books could not be made. Nor could it have been made by the American who had to label himself an American before he could even get started. Instead it is made by characters with names like Moses, or by Holocaust survivors who speak in near-halakhic terms of those who "know the terms of their contract."

These books would make it clear that Jewish literature on a par with Jewish languages can be created in English, except for one limitation. In each of Bellow's novels, all of which include these Jewish textual references, the references are nearly always taking place in the past. A late Bellow novel generally features a Jewish character whose knowledge of Jewish texts is rooted in a vanished childhood, or in a destroyed European Jewish life.

In this way, Bellow's path is surprisingly similar to Glatshteyn's. Everything is based in the world of Jewish languages of the past, with no obvious potential for the future.

Which leads us to the possibility of path number three.

Forty years ago, the American Jewish writer Cynthia Ozick proposed English as a new Jewish language, one that would follow in the chain of Jewish languages and whose resonances, as she put it, would be midrashic and liturgical. She has since renounced this idea, and it's true that it's more fantasy than anything else, the fantasy of jealous people. I'm one of them.

I began writing novels out of jealousy. I was studying Hebrew and Yiddish literature and became intensely jealous of the writers I was studying. I didn't envy the worlds they came from, but I envied their language for the ease with which that archaeology of belief rose to the surface. To me, everything that felt inauthentic about American Jewish life came from the fact that it was missing its own language. I decided that I would try to write in English as though English were a Jewish language, to write contemporary novels about largely secular people but whose words were rooted in ancient texts.

At the time I worried about all the wrong things. I worried that the exercise was artificial, without knowing that all art is artificial – that's why it's called art – and without knowing that my hunger for something deeper than what American life offered was itself a feature of American life. I worried that I was imposing something on English that it would reject like a grafted organ, without knowing that no one since Chaucer has written in "pure" English anyway, and probably not even him. Most of all, I worried that there was no audience for it – because how many people were there who would know or care what I was talking about? What I failed fully to understand was that literature is about communication, and that I had overestimated how similar readers had to be to me in order to care. My books are now available in many languages, and while I'm often on those panels I mentioned earlier, I'm also often invited to speak in churches and other settings where no one would have invited Glatshteyn. I cite this not as a victory, but as an acknowledgment that literature works on many different levels – that the author writes one book, but that everyone who reads that book is reading a different book from the one the author wrote, and sometimes they are reading a better book than the one the author wrote.

Is there such a thing as an American Jewish language, then? Should there be? I've thought about this a lot since then. There are certainly hundreds of words that I might feel free to use in certain Jewish circles but that I would never include in an article for the *Wall Street Journal*, and those words aren't Yiddish or Hebrew but something else entirely, something new. But it's worth mentioning that I also wouldn't include those words in my books, and versions of them appear only in the Hebrew translations of my books. I sometimes explain things in my books that Glatshteyn felt no need to explain, but I also don't explain very much, because I know that my readers will take what they want to take. There are layers in my books, as there are layers in all books, and readers who want to find them will.

So here, at last, is the real beauty and power and possibility of a new American Jewish language, the gift that I have inherited from both American and Jewish literature: I never need to convince anyone that I am an American writer, and I never need to deny that I am a Jewish writer – because all of my readers, no matter who they are, know the terms of the contract. And for that I owe both my tradition and my country an unending gratitude.

What Do Jews Owe America?

Norman Podhoretz

Between 1880 and 1924, nearly three million Jews fled from Eastern Europe to the United States, outnumbering by a factor of ten the roughly 300,000 Jews from Germany who had come here earlier.

These Yiddish-speaking immigrants, whose descendants would constitute the vast majority of American Jewry, called their new country *di goldeneh medineh*, "the golden land." Of course, there was no gold in the streets, as some of them seemed actually to imagine, and so they had to struggle, and struggle hard. But there was another kind of gold in America, a more precious kind than the gold of coins, the kind that gleamed through the conditions that made up what came to be known as American exceptionalism.

Ma nishtanta hamedina hazot mikol hamedinot? ("How did this land differ from all other lands?") Well, in America, to begin with, there was no trace, or any remotely functional equivalent, of the species of autocratic power that had been one of the two great enemies of the Jews of Europe from time immemorial. In Europe, autocratic governments at best extended at their own convenience a degree of toleration to the Jews living under their rule that could be, and often was, withdrawn at a moment's notice. But in the democratic republic set up in America, government acted as a bulwark against, and not an enforcer of, any form of legal discrimination against the Jews.

For America had been founded on the truly revolutionary principle that all men were created equal. This meant, in theory and to an ever-growing extent in practice, that for the first time in human history, it was not supposed to matter who your father was. Therefore Jews, if born elsewhere, had a relatively easy path to citizenship and the rights that came with it; and to any Jew born here, those rights were as much a birthright as they were to an American whose ancestors had arrived on the Mayflower. Moreover, the rights belonging to all American citizens were also declared to have come from God and to be "unalienable" – which is to say that they were immune from revocation by the state.

It was the same with the other and even greater enemy of the Jews of Europe: the Christian churches. In Europe, the churches – whether Catholic, Orthodox, or Protestant – could and did institute and enforce anti-Jewish measures. But in America, even if they wanted to harm the Jews, they lacked the power to do so, thanks to the disestablishment clause of the First Amendment, which forbade the state to favor any one religion against all the others.

But with respect to the Jews in particular, there was another, and in some ways more significant, difference between the Christianity of the European churches and the Christianity of the English Puritans who settled here in the early decades of the seventeenth century. To put it simply: the Puritans did not share in the relentless and remorseless hostility to the Jews that prevailed in the churches of Europe.

The main reason is that the Puritans felt a great affinity with the ancient Children of Israel. Thus, from the very beginning a Puritan Synod declared in no uncertain terms that "the ways of God toward this His people are in many respects like unto His dealings with Israel of old." Accordingly, like the ancient Israelites, the Puritans even made a covenant with God. "If we keep this covenant," said John Winthrop, the first governor of Massachusetts, "we shall find that the God of Israel is among us." The God, that is, of the Old Testament, not His son of the New.

Their identification with the ancient Israelites inescapably colored the Puritans' attitude to the Jews of their own time. It would be a gross exaggeration to say that they became philo-Semitic, but it would not be going too far to say that they helped to create a climate in which it was possible for Jews to feel that they had found a home in America – then and forever after.

For the influence of Puritan attitudes did not die with the Colonial era. On the contrary. Perry Miller, the great authority on American Puritanism, argues that it has come to be "one of the continuous factors in American life and thought...even though the original creed is lost."

We see this brightly reflected in today's evangelical Christian community, which bases its fervent support of Israel on verse 12:3 in the Book of Genesis where God says to Abraham of the people he will father: "I will bless them that bless thee, and curse him that curseth thee: and in thee shall all families of the earth be blessed."

But let me cite several examples of the lingering influence of the Puritan attitude toward Jews even on secular gentiles as late as the late-nineteenth century. We now know, thanks to Jonathan Sarna's book *Lincoln and the Jews: A History*, that Abraham Lincoln was one such gentile. Another was Harriet Beecher Stowe, the author of *Uncle Tom's Cabin*, who once said:

> I think no New Englander, brought up under the regime established by the Puritans, could really estimate how much of himself had actually been formed by [his] constant face-to-face intimacy with Hebrew literature.

Harriet's own husband, Calvin Stowe, was a fascinating case in point. A scholar not only of the Hebrew Bible but even of the Aramaic Talmud, he habitually wore a skullcap and was referred to by his wife as "my old rabbi." Her grandfather was another such case:

> My grandfather [at family prayers] always prayed standing.... [Those daily exercises] were Hebraistic in their form; they spoke of Zion and Jerusalem, of the God of Israel, the God of Jacob, as much as if my grandfather had been a veritable Jew.

Another telling example is the Harvard literary scholar Barrett Wendell, whom the critic Edmund Wilson describes as "the perfect type of old-fashioned snob in regard to every kind of American not of strictly Anglo-Saxon origin." Snob or not, Wendell could write:

> It is wholly possible...that the Yankee Puritan, with all his Old Testament feeling, was really, without knowing it, largely Jewish in blood.

Then there was the poet, playwright, and critic John Jay Chapman:

> There is a depth of human feeling in the Jew that no other race ever possessed. We do no more than imitate and follow it…. Compare the Greek, the Chinese, the Roman. These Jews are more human than any other men. It is the cause of the spread of their religion – for we are all adopted into Judah. The heart of the world is Jewish.

Finally, Mark Twain:

> [The Jew's] contributions to the world's list of great names in literature, science, art, music, finance, medicine, and abstruse learning are very out of proportion to the weakness of his numbers. He has made a marvelous fight in this world in all ages; and has done it with his hands tied behind him.

Of course, philo-Semitism, we have learned, has a nasty habit of turning into anti-Semitism, and so it was with Mark Twain and especially John Jay Chapman. When the mood was upon them, they were capable of lapsing into attacks upon the Jews laced with stereotypical charges that yielded nothing in their mendacious viciousness to the attitudes prevalent in Europe.

Not only that, but among their patrician contemporaries there was also plenty of out-and-out anti-Semitism unmitigated by occasional bursts of admiration for the Jews. The worst of them all was Henry Adams, the son and grandson of two American presidents and a major figure in the intellectual life of that era. "I detest [the Jews], and everything connected with them," he wrote, "and I live only and solely with the hope of seeing their demise, with all their accursed Judaism."

Nor were the pro-Jewish sentiments of Harriet Beecher Stowe and the others always reflected in practice, any more than the equal political and legal status of the Jews automatically carried over into the realm of the social. Indeed, in the years after the Civil War, various forms of discrimination began taking hold that would remain in place until the years after World War II. Hotels began adopting an open "No Jews Allowed" policy, elite schools and colleges began to institute quotas limiting the number of Jews who could be admitted, and entire professions like engineering, corporate law, and the professoriate were for all practical purposes closed to them.

All this having been stipulated, it remains true that the familiar obstacles Jews encountered in America did not rob them of the unfamiliar freedom to take advantage of the unprecedented opportunities they also encountered. To be sure, the immigrants of the first generation largely became members of a hard-pressed working class, and remained stuck there. But an astonishing percentage of their children became businessmen, doctors, lawyers, scientists, and teachers, while an even more amazing number of their grandchildren and great-grandchildren rose to important positions in the political world, and others reached comparable heights of influence in the arts and the world of ideas.

It goes without saying that Jews could not have achieved what they did in America if on the whole they had not possessed ambition, intelligence, the willingness to work hard, and the daring to take risks. In other countries where, as Mark Twain put it, the Jews had their hands tied behind their backs, none but the exceptionally talented could successfully overcome being shackled. It was only in America, where their hands were all finally untied, that not just the especially gifted but every Jew lucky enough to be here was given a fighting chance to prosper by producing whatever he had it in him to produce. Which a very large proportion of them proceeded to do, thereby amply repaying the debt they owed to America in the material realm.

However, there also was, and is, a debt in the spiritual realm, and here, it pains me to say, many, all too many, American Jews are in default. Despite the hostile turn the left has taken in recent decades toward Israel, and despite the anti-Semitism often disguised as anti-Zionism that has gone along with it, these Jews still cling obdurately to the liberalism of which they have long since made a substitute religion. Hence, they persist in looking at America through the liberal lens, and what they mainly see when they do is a system that breeds injustice and oppression rather than a complex of principles and institutions that has brought more freedom and more prosperity to more of its citizens than any other society in all of human history.

Since the Jewish community is among the greatest benefi-ciaries of these principles and institutions, one would expect it to be aligned with the forces dedicated to preserving, reinvigo-rating, and defending the traditional American system against the attacks to which it is relentlessly subjected by the left both at home and abroad. But no: to judge by how they vote, at least two-thirds of the entire Jewish community have instead made political common cause with those who are blind or indifferent or antagonistic to the infinitely precious virtues of the tradi-tional American system and some of whom wish to transform it into something radically different.

In their pious subservience to what I called the Torah of liberalism in a book I wrote a few years ago (*Why Are Jews Liberals?*), these Jews imagine that they are being nobly selfless when they denigrate what is in their own interest. But in that same book, I tried to show that, far from being noble, their attitude toward America is politically suicidal, intellectually indefensible, and morally perverse. I then concluded with the admittedly faint hope – which I confess I still force myself to entertain – that the Jewish adherents of the Torah of liberalism will finally come to recognize how far astray it has led them. For only then will they have the wherewithal to begin making good on the spiritual debt of gratitude they owe for the many blessings America has showered upon them and their fellow Jews, just as they have done in the material realm by their multifarious contributions to American life and culture, and just as the abandoned Torah of their fathers commands them to do.

The Price of Ownership for America's Jews

Jeffrey S. Gurock

Even as the battles raged during World War II, in both the European and Asian theaters of operation, in 1944 the United States Congress moved expeditiously to honor and to reward the millions of men – and thousands of women too – who were serving under arms with the Servicemen's Readjustment Act. The so-called G.I. Bill of Rights – one of the most far-reaching pieces of legislation ever passed in Washington – made available, among other emoluments to returning veterans, low-cost mortgages making home ownership affordable; a fulfillment for many of a major part of the American dream. With their loan guarantees in hand, millions of Americans made their way to bucolic suburban locales. The two Levittowns – one in Pennsylvania, the other situated just twenty-five miles east of New York City – became the most iconic communities. There, with the government's kind assistance, a couple could purchase a Cape Cod-style house for $7,500 or a ranch for $9,500 in what was then characterized as "the largest housing development ever put up by a single builder." A new era in American demography and history was underway.

America's Jews qualified en masse for the federal government's reward. More than during any prior American war, in excess of 550,000 Jews had served loyally and many courageously during the battle against Nazism, fascism, and Japanese imperialism. For many, it was their way of responding to Hitlerism – although a G.I. could not choose where he would be sent to fight. For others, it was their testimony to their allegiance to their adopted country. At the war's end, they – like so many of their fellow Americans – cashed in on their honorable discharges and joined the march out of town. Using Nassau County, Long Island – a suburb of Gotham where one of the Levittowns is located – as an example, as of 1959 this "bedroom community" housed 329,000 Jews. They constituted more than a quarter of the population.

Significantly, not only did Jews who served have the money to buy their dream homes, but this minority group was generally welcomed into these new environments. Though social anti-Semitism had its final heyday during wartime, in the decade that followed, anti-Jewish animus declined precipitously. To some extent, this change was due to Americans' revulsion over what Hitlerism had wrought. Jews also garnered noticeable street credibility from their fine efforts when the Allied democracies had been existentially challenged. But perhaps most importantly, they benefited from the beginnings of a growing respect for cultural differences. A more egalitarian-minded America in the making no longer pushed Jews to stay with their own kind. Cooperation and friendship among groups were points of emphasis in these new hometowns. Lines of ethnic demarcation and long-standing religious differences were blurred as everyone made an effort to get along. That was, so long as the prospective residents were white. African-Americans were generally restricted from settling in suburbia through either formal covenants or gentlemen's agreements and the still-discriminatory policies of the government. Commenting on this endemic situation, builder par-excellence William Levitt reportedly averred that while he was certainly in favor of civil rights, given the circumstances of the time, he could solve either a housing problem or a racial problem. He chose, like most other realtors, the former course of action. Many of the blacks who would be segregated in the interiors of cities would in time come into conflict with – among others – some of the Jews who stayed in town. But, for most Jews of the early post-war period, a new era of acceptance and comfort in America had begun.

While now a time for the fulfillment of promises started for American Jews, American Judaism suffered a critical downturn in its fortunes. The events and consequences of that day constituted the onset of the decline in identification that continues to the present moment. The most crucial loss was the Jewish neighborhood: the home for the organic, informal connections that linked Jews to each other in distinct urban environments. In prior decades, so complete had been this bonding in the sidewalk neighborhoods that a youngster could believe that "the whole world was Jewish," though statistically speaking he shared his part of the city with other ethnic groups with whom he did not have the best of relations. His Jewish universe began in the weekday morning when he attended the public schools. In these halls – at least in America's largest cities – Jewish pupils and often their teachers predominated. The Catholic youngsters around them often went to parochial schools. After the bell rang at 3 o'clock, he repaired to the Jewish-owned candy store, bakery, or meat market, where he met up and hung out with his fellows. They were part of a non-violent street club, even if the policeman on the beat might refer to them as a gang. Missing, however, in his constellations of connections was any sustained relationship to Jewish religious life. He might have played in the synagogue center's gym, but rarely if ever made it upstairs to the sanctuary, except on his wedding day when he married a neighborhood Jewish gal whom he met in a Jewish trade or occupation. On the High Holy Days, they would be among the thousands who perambulated up and down the main "Jewish streets" to see and be seen by their neighbors, perhaps stopping for a while inside the *shul* to wish a good year to a parent or grandparent.

For some Jewish suburbanites the loss of the "urban virtues" of Jewish street life was hardly a deprivation. They did not miss "the hallways or lobbies, as in apartment houses, for chance meetings" or "the elevators for quick exchange of gossip and news," and the neighborhood "corner luncheonettes for ready sociability" with those from their own background. They had been given license to live with whomever they wanted in the new environment and readily accepted the offer. Far more Jews, however, made conscious efforts to create neighborhoods within the "crabgrass frontier," even if sidewalks were not always in place. Such a determination was seen in their choice of sub-divisions within suburban expanses. Though not defined as Jewish quarters, newcomers gravitated to where their co-ethnics lived. In other words, it came down to the question of whom they would feel most comfortable living with in "courts-*culs de sac*, surrounded in circular fashion by twenty to forty garden apartments" where "privacy was at a minimum." And at the end of the day – literally and figuratively – and in the most informal of settings, they preferred being among fellow Jews.

For these Jewish adults, as much as they wanted to "live like others…and live with others," they were not fully comfortable with gentiles. Perhaps their evident reticence was born of their memories from pre-war days, of nasty Christians who cat-called Jews – and sometimes attacked them – on mean city streets. These Jews resided, consequently, on "the edge of friendliness" with those around them. At the same time, this generation unquestionably sought out formal comradeship among the Christian fellow suburbanites. Perhaps, to partially cope with their ambivalence over how to relate to their neighbors of different faiths, Jews were the consummate joiners in the get-along environment. Build a firehouse, they were proud to be on the committee. If there was a need to energize a school or library board, Jews were enthusiastic helpers. In one closely examined community, it was found that Jews were lauded for the leadership in the establishment of a Little League. Inevitably, warm friendships evolved as everyone pitched in. But when the task was completed, these Jews still resonated to a palpable allegiance – and some inherent suspicions – which they carried from the old neighborhood.

But unless a family talked explicitly – if not continually – about what was still wrong with gentiles, parents' residual anxieties were lost on their children. After all – using a sports cultural metaphor as a for instance – when a boy came to bat on a sunny Saturday afternoon on a Little League field that his parents helped finance, and quickly glanced at the bleachers, there were his mother and father cheering on his efforts along with the Christian neighbor whose son played on the same white, "integrated" team. The double-play combination of the Jewish second baseman and the gentile shortstop might also sit next to each other during the school week at the public school whose bookshelves were stocked with books that their parents had sponsored. Playing on a level social playing field, they were a world apart from the fist fighting of the slums between competing and antagonistic ethnic-allied squads. And when the game was over in suburbia, winners and losers, buddies to be sure, repaired to one or another parent's home, which only deepened their friendly relationships. Consequently, for those Jewish adults who worried about the Jewish future of their youngsters – and not all of them cared – the fear factor was that down the road intermarriages would naturally result from having Christians as their best friends. In the early 1950s, one Midwestern Jewish suburbanite publicly unburdened himself of his mixed feelings about his children's growing intimacy with gentiles. He admitted that "inevitably many [parents] maintain that the religion of the girl" their son "bring[s] home is of minor importance." But for him and his friends, intermarriage was not "an intellectual business – it is an inheritance from *Bube* and *Zeide* which outweighs liberal logic." Most pointedly, he made it clear that while in the city neighborhoods "the odds are in your favor," such is not the case in suburbia. When he was growing up, he recalled emotionally that Jews knew who they were and what they were. "Out here," he asserted, there was a need "to stack the deck." Otherwise, they would be destined to pay a deep price for all that came with owning their place in post-war America.

Accordingly in suburbia, for those who harbored such anxieties, the synagogue was called upon to be an ersatz Jewish neighborhood. Indeed, more than at any prior time in American Jewish history, it became the place where faith in the future of American Judaism resided. The mission that rabbis of all modern denominations embraced began, of course, with bringing Jews into their sanctuaries to encounter the Almighty. For Conservative rabbis in particular, the nuancing of traditional Jewish law to facilitate potential congregants to use their automobiles – the staple of suburban transportation – to approach the synagogue on holy days was for sure an effective mechanism for maximizing attendance. In pushing religiosity, theologians of all Jewish stripes had a powerful ally. An American ethos of the day hallowed its people as "one nation under God indivisible." Rabbis reasoned correctly that if Christians now believed that it was an act of American patriotism to attend "the church of their choice," Jews would follow suit. And enough worshipers did so, making for what was called "a revival of Judaism."

But trumping these laudable objectives was the call to convince young people that there was much that was special in living day by day as a Jew. Essentially, the clergy was out to reconstruct in formal, organized settings, the sensibilities of the old neighborhood, emphasizing ongoing, natural linkages among those blessed with the same heritages. The most popular vehicle for this effort, beyond preparing youngsters for their bar-mitzvahs and now the bat-mitzvahs that parents wanted – remember those *Bubes* and *Zeides* visiting from the city who had their say – were denominational youth groups and summer programs. Judaism's major institutional competition was very often the non-sectarian afternoon and vacation-time neighborhood centers; ironically, establishments that Jews helped build and support. After all, they were good neighbors. These were non-judgmental settings – not unlike the Little League or for that matter after-school dance troupes or public choirs – that brought youngsters into continuing close daily contact with each other. In some cases – in the long run – these organizations fostered life-long gender-based relationships. Through center activities, Jewish young men and women were moved naturally away from a special relationship with other Jews.

Among those who were Orthodox in suburbia, the modern Orthodox day school offered youngsters a more substantial sheltered environment. In those venues, no matter how little or how much they learned of traditional teachings and whatever their ultimate commitments to Orthodox practice, at least there they were separated during the school day from other groups and influences. However, early post-war "parochial school pupils" were a small minority among Jewish baby boomers.

In most suburban communities and within each of the Jewish streams, there were notable success stories. They were the young men and young women who found and clung to each other and committed themselves to strong identification with Judaism. In many cases, they would gravitate to the several schools of Jewish higher education for more advanced training. Arguably, they would become eventually the leaders within the generations that followed who would continue the struggle to imbue future youngsters with that special sense of group belonging that once radiated so naturally from city neighborhoods. But the vast majority of their contemporaries were unmoved by religious lures; so comfortable had they become with their place in an increasingly undifferentiated America.

They showed how willingly and how well they fit in – oblivious that any price was being paid – during the next step in their life journeys as they were accepted within America's elite secular universities. The same G.I. Bill that had brought their families to suburbia had also pried open the doors for their fathers' admission to colleges that previously had been off-limits to all but the most select Jews. During the height of the Cold War – particularly after Sputnik had frightened America into believing that it was losing the educational battle to the Soviets – the call went out to recruit our nation's "best and brightest." And Jews always did well on entrance exams. On campus – in ivy-covered neighborhoods of sorts – Jews were welcomed in. To be sure, these achievers could choose to be part of institutional Jewish life on campus. College officials – as good cultural pluralists – supported the idea that a student could be a Harvardian and a "Hillelian." And from the mid-1960s on, schools smiled on the idea that Jewish studies was a legitimate academic discipline, available to all in non-dogmatic ways, and was attractive to significant numbers of Jewish students. But notwithstanding these options, many more Jewish undergraduates – unless they were devout counter-culturalists and rejected the suburban middle-class values that they had been taught early on – naturally gravitated to diverse friendship circles within and without the classroom. These liaisons brought together contemporaries of all formerly muted ethnic backgrounds and eventually also included African-Americans in the mix.

Eventually, as maturing adults – with sheepskins and job offers in hand – many of these Jews returned to the city. They made good the prediction that the eminent economist John Kenneth Galbraith had made in the early 1970s when he opined that once "the suburban movement" had run its course "the superior quality of city life will assert itself." However, when this generation of gentrifiers reoccupied metropolises – as they have over the last quarter century or more – they did not seek to reify the sights, sounds, and emotions of their parents' old neighborhood, even if some were domiciled in co-ops or condominiums only paces away from where their ancestors had resided. Perhaps, on walking tours, they would be enthused for a moment if they saw an image on a rehabilitated building that still had its original Hebrew letters on its frontage. But, in so many places, "urban homesteaders" were simply willing to pay the price to turn dismal districts into "delightful neighborhoods" full of "colorful shops and restaurants," emblematic of the sort of life they wanted to lead. But the need to be among other Jews was low on the list of their desires as they calculated where to live.

Using Gotham, America's largest Jewish city – and the one that I have studied most – as an example, it became clear as early as the 1980s that a new generation of the well-educated and economically successful did not sense that its whole world was Jewish or desire that it be so. If anything, the whole city was their undifferentiated neighborhood. In fact, when surveyed at that point in time, close to half indicated that their closest friends were not Jewish. Some, however, did maintain one long-standing tradition that had been widely observed back in their parents' day. Some of these Jews could be found promenading around their neighborhoods in their best finery on Rosh HaShana, a day which is almost a civic holiday. But their crowd likely included non-Jewish friends and, increasingly, relatives. They are comfortable with acceptance and gratified to own more than a piece of America's economic and cultural life. Given this mindset, those who are today concerned with Jewish continuity are challenged to convince these Jews that they have lost an important part of their identities, the most preliminary step in effectuating interest in any and all things Jewish.[2]

---

2. Note: The primary sources that undergird this analysis, highlighted as quoted statements, can be found noted in the following books that I have written which expand on the power and problems of neighborhood life in urban areas and suburbs. See Jeffrey S. Gurock, *Judaism's Encounter with American Sports*, ch. 6; *Orthodox Jews in America*, ch. 9; *Jews in Gotham: New York Jews in a Changing City*, chs. 2 and 6; and *Jewish Harlem: The Birth, Decline and Revival of an Urban Jewish Community*.

Jewish Artists and the American Way

Tevi Troy

American Jews, and particularly American Jewish
entertainers, have made an enormous contribution to this great
country. In nearly all of the major artistic fields, there are examples of disproportionate and crucial involvement by American
Jews. A quick review of the major fields of entertainment reveals
the high level of Jewish influence.

The Jewish impact in Hollywood can be seen in this
sophomoric yet revealing exchange at the 2013 Oscar ceremony. Ted the talking teddy bear told Mark Wahlberg, "I was
born Theodore Shapiro and I would like to donate money
to Israel and continue to work in Hollywood forever. Thank
you, I'm Jewish." To this, Wahlberg – who is not Jewish –
responded, "You're an idiot," to which Ted replied, "Yeah,
well, we'll see who the idiot is when they give me a private
plane at the next secret synagogue meeting." In another
moment of Hollywood's recognition of its Jewishness, at the

2010 Academy Awards ceremony, Steve Martin suggested that Christoph Waltz's Jew-hunting Nazi character in the film *Inglourious Basterds* should have taken his search for Jews to the Oscars, looking around the room and calling it "the mother lode."

When it comes to literature, as far back as 1969 Nobel and Pulitzer Prize-winning novelist Saul Bellow lamented "this tendency to turn [Bernard] Malamud, [Philip] Roth, and me into the Hart, Schaffner & Marx of American literature." As for comedy, Lawrence Epstein's *The Haunted Smile* reveals the remarkable statistic that a few decades ago one survey found that 80 percent of American comedians were Jewish. With respect to Broadway, Jewish prevalence on both sides of the stage is long-standing. The pervasiveness of Jews in theater is so great that the Monty Python musical *Spamalot* even included a seemingly extraneous Jewish character, whose presence in the show was specifically to enable a song called "You Won't Succeed on Broadway (If You Don't Have Any Jews)."

I could go on, but the point is clear. One need not belabor the issue – nor give additional grist to anti-Semites[1] – to demonstrate that Jews have had a remarkable run in the entertainment sphere in modern American life.

What's most noteworthy about all of this success is how little of it we saw before the twentieth century. Nobody thought that Jews dominated nineteenth-century theater or literature. For most of the two thousand years of exile from Judea, Jewish intellectual efforts went into creating the Talmud and other great works of Jewish law and textual interpretation. Given this

---

1. Recall the joke about the Jew who used to read the anti-Semitic press because it was filled with good news: the Jews control the banks, the Jews control the media, the Jews control Hollywood...

remarkable flourishing of Jews in America, especially over the last century or so, the question is why.

The answer to this question gets to the heart of the issue of what America owes the Jews and, in doing so, brings us closer to an understanding of how the Jewish community has successfully paid back this great nation. The fact of the matter is that America did not make the Jews into successful entertainers. Instead, it gave the Jews an environment in which their natural talents could flourish. As a recent article in the *Economist* observed, "Jews have rarely had to choose between their American and Jewish identities: that has been one secret of America's success." It has been a secret of Jewish success as well.

Interestingly, the encouragement of the Jews has taken place at the highest levels, and for longer than most people think. In fact, in many ways, presidential leadership has helped the Jews attain their status in American life. Many are familiar with George Washington's famous letter to the Hebrew Congregation of Newport, Rhode Island, in which he wrote, "Every one shall sit in safety under his own vine and fig tree, and there shall be none to make him afraid." This message of tolerance indicated that the Jews would have a happy home in America, free of the government-based discrimination that they had experienced in nearly all of their other post-exilic stopping points.

But Washington was not the only early president with philo-Semitic tendencies. James Madison studied Hebrew at Princeton so that he could have a better understanding of the Bible and its teachings. John Quincy Adams wrote favorably about the Hebrew prophets in letters to his son, and considered writing a history of the Jewish people in his post-presidency. That project, alas, never came to fruition.

The first president to encourage an American Jewish artist was James Monroe. In 1817, Monroe visited Charleston,

South Carolina, where he saw *Alberti*, a *Romeo and Juliet*-esque drama by the Jewish playwright Isaac Harby. *Alberti* appears to have been the first fictional work by an American Jewish author that a US president read or saw. Furthermore, it is possible that Monroe saw the play specifically because of the author's identity. A few years earlier, Harby had complained in a letter to then Secretary of State Monroe about Monroe's role in the dismissal of the Jewish US Consul to Tunis, Mordecai Manuel Noah. According to the historian Jacob Rader Marcus, Monroe's attendance at Harby's play may have even been to serve as an apology to Harby for Monroe's role in firing Noah. Either way, the Monroe visit was an important early gesture in validating the work of an American Jewish artist.

The rest of the nineteenth century did not see many more such gestures, in part because the explosion of Jews into the arts did not really begin until the twentieth century. Even so, Abraham Lincoln showed some interest in Jews in the arts, seeing at least three plays with Jewish content in the years 1864 and 1865: *Gamea; or The Jewish Mother* (twice), *Leah, the Forsaken*, and Shakespeare's *The Merchant of Venice*. *Gamea* was about a kidnapped Jewish child raised as a Christian, inspired by the 1859 Mortara Affair in Italy; *Leah* was about anti-Semitism in eighteenth-century Austria.

In the twentieth century, interactions between presidents and Jewish artists became far more common. One of the most notable of these was a collaboration between Theodore Roosevelt and the British Jewish playwright Israel Zangwill. Zangwill took the name and inspiration for his play *The Melting Pot* from Roosevelt's professed views on the need to assimilate new immigrants to America. Zangwill dedicated the play to Roosevelt as well. Roosevelt even attended the 1908 Washington premiere of Zangwill's play, declaring after the performance, "It's a great play, Mr. Zangwill; it's a great play!"

As the twentieth century progressed, American Jewish artists got into the act in greater numbers. In 1915, theater fan Woodrow Wilson – he saw 250 plays as president – invited the Jewish performer Al Jolson to the White House. Jolson told the president, "I'm Al Jolson, and I want to see the president." Wilson acknowledged that he was the president, but also that he had never seen Jolson in action. Jolson did not have to be asked twice, saying, "Wait a minute – you ain't heard nothin' yet." He then sang his song "You Made Me Love You" in front of the president of the United States, a bold move that it is hard to imagine a Jewish performer replicating at the time in front of the Czar, the Kaiser, or the Queen of England. Jolson would later prove that his interests in presidential politics were not only on the Democratic side of the aisle. In 1920, he wrote and performed "Harding, He's the Man for Us" on behalf of Republican presidential nominee Warren G. Harding. In 1924, he performed, but did not write, "Keep Cool and Keep Coolidge" on behalf of sitting president Calvin Coolidge, also a Republican. Both men won their respective elections.

Jewish political involvement continued among Democrats as well. Franklin D. Roosevelt made liberal use of Jewish entertainers in his political campaigns, with Jewish stars such as Boris Karloff, Melvyn Douglas, and Edward G. Robinson among those lending their names in support of Roosevelt. Roosevelt also played an important role in cementing the standing of cinema – a highly Jewish medium – in American culture. Roosevelt understood cinema's potential to unify a large and disparate nation, and used cinema to great political effect. He ordered the creation of a White House movie theater, appeared in more movies – both fiction and nonfiction – than any other president, and encouraged the use of film in the propaganda battle against Germany. In helping to validate the important role of film in American culture, Roosevelt was also implicitly validating the role of Jews in American film, and effectively in American culture as well.

In the postwar years, Jews no longer needed the same level of validation. The war against Nazism helped discredit anti-Semitism in both polite and non-polite society, and the role of Jews expanded throughout American society. This was especially so in American culture. The emergence of television, another medium with a large Jewish presence, helped further the concept of, and comfort with, Jews in the arts. President Dwight Eisenhower was a huge fan of television, watching so regularly that a White House usher complained of the degree to which "the new vogue for television dictated certain aspects of life in the Eisenhower White House."

Eisenhower even had a role in the Jewish comedian Phil Silvers getting his role as lead in the eponymous *Phil Silvers Show*. A pre-show Silvers had the opportunity to perform before Eisenhower and other Washington luminaries at the 1954 White House Correspondents' dinner. Silvers was a hit, cracking up Eisenhower and the rest of the crowd with a routine where he looks around the room full of Washington luminaries and, after a painfully long silence, asks, "So who's minding the store?" One of the other attendees that night was a CBS executive who was so impressed with Silvers that he helped Silvers get his own show.

Eisenhower's successor, John F. Kennedy, had his own interactions with Jewish celebrities. Kennedy did not watch nearly as much television as Ike, but he was a fan of the *Jack Benny Show*, another Jewish-hosted show. He also, like Roosevelt, enlisted celebrities to back his 1960 campaign, including Tony Curtis, born Bernard Schwartz. But Kennedy's importance was more pronounced in promoting the role of Jewish writers. He had two Jewish speechwriters, Ted Sorenson and Richard Goodwin, and his White House intellectual Arthur Schlesinger had Jewish ancestry. Sorenson is presumed to have ghostwritten *Profiles in Courage*, Kennedy's pre-presidency Pulitzer Prize-winning book. Schlesinger's book about the Kennedy administration, *A Thousand Days*, would also win a Pulitzer. Kennedy also actively enlisted the support of American intellectuals, many of whom were Jewish. In his first memoir, *Making It*, Norman Podhoretz credits the Kennedy administration with raising the status of American intellectuals, noting that "from having carried a faint aura of disreputability, the title 'intellectual' all at once became an honorific."

One president who may have set back the cause of Jewish artists was Richard Nixon. His enemies list included Jewish actors such as Barbra Streisand, Paul Newman, and Tony Randall. The Nixon tapes also reveal him saying ugly things about Jews, such as repeating an observation from the Catholic Hollywood writer Paul Keyes that on "every show in Hollywood…eleven out of the twelve writers are Jewish." Both the tapes and the list were manifestations of the private Nixon. In public, though, he was more supportive, especially in having a prominent Jewish speechwriter – and later *New York Times* columnist – William Safire. Still, given his negative attitudes toward many Jewish artists, it would be hard to say that overall Nixon advanced the acceptance of Jewish artists in American life.

Nixon notwithstanding, in the post-World War II period, American presidents repeatedly honored Jewish artists with the Presidential Medal of Freedom. So many Jewish artists – under both Republican and Democratic administrations – would receive this prestigious award that the Jewishness of certain recipients became a regular and not even particularly noteworthy phenomenon. Starting with President Kennedy's 1963 configuration of the nation's highest civilian honor in its current incarnation, a host of Jewish artists – including Irving Berlin (1977), Aaron Copland (1964), Kirk Douglas (1981), Bob Dylan (2012), Vladimir Horowitz (1986), Artur Rubinstein (1976), Isaac Stern (1992), and Elie Wiesel (1992) – have won the award. These awards served as a validation of the American Jewish experience at the presidential level. Their frequency even showed that presidential approbation was no longer required for Jews to succeed artistically in America.

Even though American Jewish artists may no longer have needed presidential support, the interactions between the two continued fairly regularly. These interactions have reached a new level during the pop-culture-heavy Obama administration. Obama has been ground-breaking in his use of non-traditional media to get his message across, and Jewish artists have been an important part of this effort. In the 2008 presidential campaign, when Hollywood overwhelmingly and unabashedly backed Obama, support for Obama even became a form of performance art. During that campaign, the Jewish comedienne Sarah Silverman engaged in what she called "The Great Schlep" southward. The Great Schlep was an effort to have young Jews go down to Florida to encourage their elderly Jewish grandparents to vote for Obama, whom Silverman called "the goodest person we've ever had as a presidential choice."

As president, Obama also encouraged faux-news comedy shows, particularly *The Daily Show*, hosted by the Jewish comedian Jon Stewart. Obama appeared on the show seven times as president, a striking figure given that prior to Obama, no sitting president had ever before appeared on a late-night talk show. Obama not only made regular appearances on the late-night network shows, but did cable comedy such as Stewart's show as well. And Obama's relationship with Stewart went beyond the professional; they were apparently friends as well. Stewart visited the White House numerous times during the Obama presidency, and on one occasion they ate nachos and watched the comic film *King Ralph* together.

Obama's willingness to use non-traditional media to reach receptive but disengaged voters was a recurring theme of his presidency, and Jewish artists helped him along the way. Obama was also the first president to be interviewed on a podcast. His second podcast interview, on the show *WTF*, was with the Jewish comedian Marc Maron. Obama made news on the show by using the N-word, but he also talked explicitly about his strategy of using alternative media to reach liberal-minded listeners who aren't necessarily politically inclined. During the interview, he told Maron that he asked his communications team, "How do we talk to folks who are not already dug in in their politics?"

Another trend related to Jewish artists and Obama was the habit of Jewish White House guests giving the non-Jewish president Jewish-themed books. In the spring of 2012, the Jewish journalist Jeffrey Goldberg gave Obama *The New American Haggadah*, a collaboration between the writers Nathan Englander and Jonathan Safran Foer. The author Peter Beinart then brought not one but two copies of his get-tough-on-Israel book, *The Crisis of Zionism*, to a meeting with Obama. Obama responded by telling Beinart, who had been criticized within the Jewish community for the book, to "hang in there." (Bibi Netanyahu, somewhat more pointedly, gave Obama the *Book of Esther*, about a Persian plot to destroy the Jewish people; at an earlier point, he gave Obama Mark Twain's *Innocents Abroad* – "perhaps insensitively," in the words of former Ambassador Michael Oren.) This continuing comfort that Jews are showing with the presidents, both in their boldness, and in their literary selections, demonstrates a further step forward in the progression discussed above, that presidents have now become comfortable with American Jewish artists not only as Americans, but in their Jewish capacities as well.

Today, we often take it for granted that American Jews have a happy and comfortable home in America. As noted above, some of that comfort derives from Jewish success in the arts. As writers, actors, producers, directors, and comedians – especially comedians – Jewish Americans are well represented and at the top of their fields. This association of American Jews and entertainers has not always been a natural one, as it took some time for Jews to feel comfortable in America, as well as for Jews to gain acceptance in the larger community. But today that acceptance has arrived, and one often overlooked aspect of it is the role that our political leaders – and particularly the American presidents – have played in making it happen.

Abraham Lincoln and the Jews: A Conversation with Jonathan Sarna

The May 31, 2015 conference concluded with an interview of **Jonathan Sarna**, *professor of American Jewish history at Brandeis University and author of* Lincoln and the Jews: A History. *The interview was conducted by* **Meir Soloveichik**.

Meir Soloveichik: If there is anyone who, for American Jewish history, has helped maintain the bond between past, present, and future, it is the distinguished scholar we welcome back to Shearith Israel this evening. Jonathan Sarna is the Joseph H. and Belle R. Braun Professor of American Jewish history at Brandeis and chief historian of the National Museum of American Jewish History in Philadelphia. He has written, edited, or co-edited more than thirty books, of which the most recent, and the one we are celebrating here, is *Lincoln and the Jews: A History.*

So let me start with the obvious question. More books are written every year on Abraham Lincoln than on almost any other figure in history. But is it so clear that Lincoln was the most important person in American history – more important than, say, George Washington? Widening the lens, was he more important for the course of world history than such figures as Napoleon, or Alexander the Great, or Winston Churchill? Why the almost unique fascination with Lincoln in general, and why from a Jewish perspective in particular?

Jonathan Sarna: It's a fine question. Take the case of Washington and Napoleon. We're familiar with this story: the story of the great general who becomes a great political leader. It goes back to Joshua. But Lincoln's story is different: he's a figure who came out of nowhere, who was probably illiterate in his young life, who later went on to lose several elections – and who only then became what he became. That story is deeply inspiring – in a wholly different way.

But as for who most changed the world, one would be hard-pressed to name anyone who changed the American world, and not just the American world, more than did Lincoln. And here I can cite the testimony of a European Jew. In an essay reflecting on his own childhood, the great scholar Solomon Schechter recalls hearing about Lincoln in Romania as a child – and what a wondrous thing it was to him that a person who came from nothing and nowhere could climb so high and achieve so much.

Nor, for Schechter, did all this have anything to do with the Jews or with the story of Lincoln and the Jews. His essay shows no knowledge of that side of things. But it does touchingly bear on why people all over the world were and remain so impressed with Lincoln, the simple person from a simple background who emerges as president of his country and radically transforms it for the better.

Meir Soloveichik: I wonder whether there isn't something Jewish about precisely that point. Rabbi Jonathan Sacks points to the story of Moses in the Bible as a kind of literary antitype. Many ancient tales of heroes feature the child of a god or a king who is raised by a peasant and in time discovers his true identity and true destiny. By contrast, Moses is the child of slaves, is raised in the king's palace, rebels, and becomes a great leader. Could this quality be what attracts Jews in particular to the Lincoln story?

Jonathan Sarna: Yes, in a way. More specifically, I think that many Jews also saw in Lincoln a fellow outsider: one who became, as they aspired to become, a kind of ultimate insider. That, too, is a Jewish story. And Jews saw in Lincoln something else as well – aspects of the archetypal righteous prophet.

Meir Soloveichik: That brings us to the matter of Lincoln's relations with actual Jews. Born in Kentucky, Abraham Lincoln moves to Illinois, works as a lawyer, gets involved in politics – and meets Jews. Eventually, as you say in your book, he will become the first president actually to have Jewish friends.

Jonathan Sarna: By far the most important of his early Jewish connections was Abraham Jonas: another Abraham, this one from an upstanding Orthodox family. After the loss of his wife, Jonas moved from Cincinnati first to Kentucky and then to Illinois, became a lawyer, and through this shared profession met Abraham Lincoln. It's clear that theirs was a significant friendship; many letters were exchanged between them, and they traveled together. One of the things I was happy to discover was that Jonas's son, who lived in New Orleans, worked with Lincoln to free an African-American from Illinois who had come south, been imprisoned, and was going to be sold into slavery until freed by their joint effort and enabled to return to Illinois.

Biographers have tended to scant this friendship, but it was no minor thing. The larger point is Abraham Lincoln had a Jewish friend, and when you have a friend who's a Jew you tend to develop friendly feelings toward Jews in general; it's the same when you have a friend who's black, or Muslim, and so forth. This is a well-established sociological fact, and it helps explain at least in part why, later on, Lincoln had numerous other Jewish acquaintances.

But back to Jonas, who was something of a political genius. Indeed, he played a role in Lincoln's nomination at the 1860 Republican national convention in Chicago. William Seward had arranged to pack the hall, ensuring that when his name was proposed, an enormous demonstration would erupt, thus ensuring his own bid to head the Republican ticket. Learning of Seward's plan, Jonas said, in effect, "I can play that game, too," and arranged a similar ovation for Lincoln. If you read the proceedings of the convention, you can follow the unfolding drama. Seward failed to win on the first ballot, was abandoned by many of his supporters, and Lincoln took the third ballot.

Incidentally, among those rounded up by Jonas for his counter-demonstration was a contingent of non-Republican outsiders, including some Jews. Chicago politics never changes.

Meir Soloveichik: And so Lincoln was elected in 1860. But it seems that at the time, some of the most prominent rabbis and Jewish leaders in America didn't support him. Nor were all of them opposed to slavery. And this went from Reform to Orthodox.

Jonathan Sarna: The most famous example is Rabbi Morris Raphall, the first glamour rabbi in American Jewish history. He was then rabbi of B'nai Jeshurun synagogue in Manhattan, which in 1825 had broken away from Shearith Israel. It was a very significant congregation.

Now, many of the members of B'nai Jeshurun had business ties to the South. If you were a clothing manufacturer in those days, the cotton for your cloth came from the South. So the last thing many of them wanted was a war, which is understandable: war could be bad for business. Some of them felt the most important thing was to preserve the Union, and Raphall had the idea of finding a compromise on the slavery issue that would conduce to that end.

There was a big debate at the time about, in particular, biblical slavery. Raphall was the first to come out and say, point blank, that yes, there was slavery in the Bible, but that biblical slavery was much more humane than slavery in the American South.

Meir Soloveichik: For instance, if you wound your Israelite slave, he goes free. And of course he also goes free after six years of service.

Jonathan Sarna: Exactly. Raphall used the example of biblical slavery to argue for a middle ground between American slavery as then practiced in the South and outright abolition. This defense of some form of slavery was reported across the length and breadth of the United States, for here was a rabbi who knew Hebrew and could be credited with an authoritative reading of the Old Testament. One Southern newspaper proclaimed that it was as if Moses himself had come down from Mount Sinai to confirm and justify the Bible's "defense" of slavery. Obviously, abolitionists didn't agree.

To be sure, Jews were hardly of one mind on the matter. David Einhorn, another prominent rabbi, then in Baltimore, argued the abolitionist side in a debate with Raphall. The lawyer Abram Dittenhoefer, a young supporter of the Republican party who had grown up in the South, had been pro-slavery, and had undergone a conversion to the anti-slavery cause after coming to New York, became one of that cause's most effective and influential spokesmen. And then I might parenthetically mention Michael Heilprin, another of Raphall's opponents, who retorted sarcastically that in addition to slavery, the Bible permits concubinage and polygamy, so perhaps Raphall should urge that these be brought back as well.

Wherever they lived, north or south, Jews tended to follow their non-Jewish neighbors – which could sometimes get them into trouble. A prominent example here is that of Isaac Mayer Wise, one of the most important figures in American Reform Judaism and a prolific writer. An antiwar Democrat, he lived in Cincinnati – just across the Ohio River from Kentucky, a slave state. Many of his readers and followers kept slaves. Wise had very little good to say about Abraham Lincoln – until Lincoln was assassinated, whereupon he executed a complete 180-degree turn.

Unlike Wise, Raphall, who also thought Lincoln's election was a disaster, was staunchly pro-Union. Both of his children fought for the Union, and one lost an arm. In another telling vignette, Raphall's son-in-law, C.M. Levy, was appointed assistant quartermaster in the Union army. Upon recommending him for the position, Lincoln wrote, "We have not yet appointed a Hebrew," making this the first case of affirmative action for a Jew in American history. Lincoln's letter to Secretary of War Edwin M. Stanton, dated November 4, 1862, is in the Shapell Manuscript Collection.

Incidentally, the president also went on to write of Levy: He "is well vouched, as a capable and faithful man." This was a characteristic bit of Lincolnian wordplay, intimating that Levy would be faithful to the Union because he was a faithful Orthodox Jew. And indeed that quality distinguished Levy from earlier Jewish appointees of Lincoln's, all of whom were assimilated. In naming Levy, who was known to be Orthodox, Lincoln was naming someone who would not "only" be a token representative of the Jews.

Meir Soloveichik: Of course, we know that Jews fought for the South as well. There's the famous story about a Jewish Union soldier, in the last year of the war, who is looking for a place to join a Seder. He's already in the occupied South. Seeing a child eating matza on the front steps of a house, he asks for some. The child runs into the house and calls out to his mother, "Ma, there is a damn Yankee Jew outside."

If you were a Union Jew, or if you were a Southern Jew, what would you be thinking through the lens of your Judaism?

Jonathan Sarna: In many ways, the Civil War – and not World War I, which is the conflict we usually think of in this connection – is the first time you find Jews fighting Jews, and conscious of that fact. Conscious, that is, both of their ties to their fellow Jews who happened to inhabit a different part of the country and conscious that some Jews were their enemy.

Some worked hard to maintain ties to both sides. The famous Philadelphia philanthropist Rebecca Gratz, who by this time was very old, had grandnephews on either side. As she herself never married, she regarded her brother's grandchildren as her own. She wrote to them all, anxious to let them know that she loved them no matter which side they were on.

Then you had others whose political loyalties destroyed personal ties. Some of the children of Abraham Jonas, who had as much as recommended that Southerners be hanged, fought for the North; but others had moved to New Orleans and, breaking their father's heart, ended up fighting for the cause he was convinced was absolutely wrong.

Meir Soloveichik: Getting back to Lincoln, can you tell us about his chiropodist, and about that gentleman's importance for the events and personalities we're discussing?

Jonathan Sarna: An amazing figure. Issachar Zacharie was what we would today call a podiatrist. Jews played a totally disproportionate role in the development of that branch of medicine partly because they couldn't get into other branches; chiropody, being looked down upon as a profession, was easier to break into. Even in England, the royal family's chiropodists for several generations were Jews.

Zacharie was by far the most important chiropodist of his day. Nobody exactly knows how or by what method, but he was able to lessen foot pain and provide sufferers with greater comfort. Like many chiropodists, he also treated other ailments. At one point he treated Lincoln for a strained wrist.

Zacharie enjoyed a huge reputation. His ads were everywhere. Among his patients was the poet William Cullen Bryant, who like Lincoln was a fanatical walker. When the Civil War started, Bryant wrote to Lincoln – we have the letter – recommending Zacharie and suggesting that the military hire a corps of chiropodists for the benefit of the fighting men. Bryant thought that Lincoln, who had famously painful feet, should have Zacharie take personal charge of the corps. Although that particular idea never came to fruition, the president enlisted

Zacharie's services for himself, and the two developed a friendship. After the recapture of New Orleans, Lincoln sent Zacharie there to win back the affections of its Jews to the Union. While there, he was also involved in what we would call *shtadlanut*: lobbying for Jewish causes and trying to help Jews who'd been arrested or were otherwise in trouble. At the same time, he also served as a kind of spy for Lincoln, sending back reports on what he observed.

Plenty of people distrusted Zacharie. Having read all of the material, I still can't say with certainty whether Lincoln was right to put his trust in him. There's at least one ingratiating letter from the chiropodist to Judah Benjamin, the Confederacy's secretary of state, in which, although it's clear that the writer supports Benjamin personally, it's still uncertain whether his motive as a spy was to sniff out possible grounds for a peace agreement or whether he was double-dealing.

Until more evidence comes in – and I'm not sure it will – we won't know. For now, what we do know is that we have here another fascinating example of Lincoln turning to a Jewish friend in the hope both that he will affect the attitudes of his fellow Jews and, possibly, that he might even be able to make peace by talking to one particular fellow Jew, Benjamin, in hopes that the two would find some way of narrowing differences.

No less fascinating is that in 1864, when Lincoln runs for reelection, Zacharie strongly supports him; not only that, but – and this is really the beginning of Jewish group politics – he rallies American Jews to vote for the president. He goes so far as to write reassuringly to Lincoln that he's organized it all and that the Jews will vote as arranged. In the event, Lincoln's margin of victory in 1864 was much greater than expected, which no doubt had more to do with other votes than those of the Jews; still, Zacharie was a very happy man.

The lesson: the prevailing assumption among most historians that American Jewish political activism begins in the twentieth century is completely wrong.

Meir Soloveichik: You note in your book that on July 4, 1863, which was a Sabbath, the rabbi of the Mikveh Israel synagogue in Philadelphia, Sabato Morais, gave a sermon ending with the following plea to the Almighty: "Encircle Pennsylvania with Thy mighty shield. Protect the lives of our inhabitants." At the time, Pennsylvania was where the fighting was going on, most ferociously at Gettysburg. In his sermon, Morais referred to the release of the Declaration of Independence on July 4, 1776 as "the event which four score and seven years ago brought to this new world, light and joy."

So did Lincoln just steal that phrase, "four score and seven years ago," from the rabbi?

Jonathan Sarna: Not only was the battle of Gettysburg fought on that day, July 4, but, unusually, July 4 that year also coincided with the fast day of the Seventeenth of Tammuz.

Meir Soloveichik: As did July 4, 1776.

Jonathan Sarna: So Morais is in Philadelphia, not so far away, as the crow flies, from Gettysburg. Nobody knows how the battle will end. He asks, will it be the Seventeenth of Tammuz? – meaning, will the Confederacy win? – or will it be July 4? – meaning, will the Union win? And it's in that connection that he invokes the event that occurred "four score and seven years ago."

All Lincoln biographers have wondered where Lincoln got that line. Of course the model for it occurs in the King James translation of Psalms, but there the span is three score and ten, not four score and seven. Different conjectures have been put forth, and it's certain that Lincoln knew his Psalms very well. But this sermon marks the first time that the phrase "four score and seven" is used in connection specifically with the battle of Gettysburg.

As it happens, quite a few Morais sermons were sent to the White House. I can't prove that this one was ever among them; the White House acknowledged receipt of several others, but not this one. It was a great sermon, too. It couldn't have been well prepared in advance, because the battle had just gotten under way. In any event, it was published in the *Jewish Messenger*, and I think it's plausible that Lincoln or somebody else noted the phrase and, as it were, highlighted it with a yellow marker. To my mind it's not impossible, and it offers a much better answer to the question of where the phrase came from than any of the others that have been put forward.

Meir Soloveichik: A final question. Isaac Mayer Wise, he of the 180-degree turn, claimed after the assassination that Abraham Lincoln was Jewish and that Lincoln had told him so. It's clearly not true. So was Wise overcome by emotion and did he believe it, or was he just making it up?

Jonathan Sarna: At the time, Benjamin Szold – the father of Henrietta Szold, founder of the women's organization Hadassah and much else – then a rabbi in Baltimore, insisted the contrary; and Szold spent much more time with Lincoln than Wise ever did. But Wise did have a tendency to declare people Jewish.

I'm not prepared to say that he was lying, and who knows what Lincoln may have whispered to him on some occasion? But then why hadn't Wise reported it earlier, and why did he wait until Lincoln was no longer alive?

Incidentally, Wise was hardly alone in claiming that certain well-known or beloved figures had Jewish roots. You can find this sort of stuff on the Internet. Some Jews made the name Roosevelt out to be Jewish ("Rosenvelt"), and lately there've been rumors that Lyndon Johnson was a Jew. The impulse tells you more about Jews than about Roosevelt or Johnson, and it's in that spirit that we should take Isaac Mayer Wise.

Lincoln did not know much about his ancestors. I have no doubt that they were Christians profoundly shaped by the Hebrew Bible, and in that sense "Hebraic," but as you say there's no evidence whatsoever that he was Jewish – notwithstanding all of the websites devoted to proving it. What's really impressive is how much love for Lincoln is evidenced by these persistent rumors and theories.

Meir Soloveichik: On that note, a final-final point. In your book, you stress how Lincoln's language grows more and more religious as time goes on, especially and most famously in the Second Inaugural, where he basically creates a theology of the Civil War and indeed of America. In that connection, you stress that the language he comes to employ is less Christian than universal, or universal with a Hebraic tinge. Can you reflect briefly on Lincoln's religious vision of America and what it means for the connection between Jews and the American idea and the home they found here?

Jonathan Sarna: This to my mind is the deep significance of Lincoln – namely, that he embraces Jews as equals in America and as equals in the American idea. It's because of Lincoln that the military chaplaincy will become a chaplaincy for all denominations and not only for Christians. That was in itself a sign that Jews were emphatically not to be considered second-class citizens.

In his First Inaugural, Lincoln had made a Christological reference, to which some Jews protested. I think he learned from that. At Gettysburg, where after all many Jewish soldiers also fell, he spoke of "this nation under God" – an all-embracing phrase very different from the Christological language employed by Edward Everett in his own endless speech at Gettysburg, which ignored the fact that Jews had fallen there.

And it's not a matter of a single phrase. As you observe, in the Second Inaugural he develops an entire theological vocabulary, previously non-existent, in which America is at once deeply religious but not narrowly Christian. We cannot underestimate how significant that is for the place of Jews in America.

This hardly means that Lincoln's legacy went unchallenged. A man like Andrew Johnson, who succeeded him in the presidency, had no interest in this sort of thing. Although he was careful to make sure that the ceremony commemorating Lincoln wouldn't coincide with the Christian Pentecost, Johnson refused to change the date when it fell on Shavuot.

So it's not linear, but the Lincoln tradition – the all-embracing tradition that says that Jews are by definition part of America – is the tradition that won. It's hard to exaggerate how transformational this was and is. Jews in America, thanks to Lincoln, are insiders. Of how many other countries could Jews ever make such a claim?

Contributors

Jeffrey S. Gurock is Libby M. Klaperman Professor of Jewish History at Yeshiva University. He is the author or editor of eighteen books, including *Jews in Gotham: New York Jews in a Changing City, 1920-2010* which was awarded the Everett Prize by the Jewish Book Council as the best non-fiction Jewish book in 2012. His most recent books are *Jews of Harlem: The Rise, Decline and Revival of an Urban Jewish Community* and *Constant Challenge: Sports and American Judaism.*

Dara Horn is the author of four novels, of which the latest, *A Guide for the Perplexed*, was selected for *Booklist*'s Best Books of 2013 and longlisted for the Carnegie Medal for Excellence in Fiction. She is currently a visiting professor in Jewish studies at Harvard, where she teaches Yiddish and Hebrew literature.

Norman Podhoretz served as editor-in-chief of *Commentary* from 1960 until his retirement in 1995. He is the author of twelve books, including *My Love Affair with America* and *Why Are Jews Liberals?*. In 2004 he was awarded the Presidential Medal of Freedom.

Rick Richman, founder of the blog *Jewish Current Issues*, writes for *Commentary*, the *American Thinker*, the *Jewish Journal*, the *Tower*, and other publications. His current project is a book about the trips to America of Chaim Weizmann, Vladimir Jabotinsky, and David Ben-Gurion during the opening months of World War II.

Jonathan Sarna is the Joseph H. & Belle R. Braun Professor of American Jewish History at Brandeis University and chief historian of the National Museum of American Jewish History. He has written, edited, or co-edited more than thirty books. The most recent, co-authored with Benjamin Shapell, is *Lincoln and the Jews: A History*.

Meir Soloveichik is the rabbi of Congregation Shearith Israel in New York and director of the Straus Center for Torah and Western Thought of Yeshiva University.

Tevi Troy is a presidential historian and former White House aide. He is the author of *What Jefferson Read, Ike Watched, and Obama Tweeted: 200 Years of Popular Culture in the White House*.

The fonts used in this book are from the Garamond family

The Toby Press publishes fine writing
on subjects of Israel and Jewish interest.
For more information, visit www.tobypress.com.